What's My Pa$sw0Rd?

Corbett Speciale

TEKEASE PRESS / Peoria

Published by TEKEASE PRESS, Peoria, Illinois
TEKEASE PRESS™ and TEKEASE ON-SITE® are trademarks of TEKEASE ON-SITE®. All other trademarks are the property of their respective owners.

Printed in the United States of America

Library of Congress Cataloging-in-Publication Data available upon request.

ISBN 978-1482629712

First Edition

$\mathscr{L}$egalese and Disclaimers.

This book is presented solely for educational and entertainment purposes. The author and publisher are not offering it as legal, information security, or professional advice. While best efforts have been used in preparing this book, the author and publisher make no representations or warranties of any kind and assume no liabilities of any kind with respect to the accuracy or completeness of the contents and specifically disclaim any implied warranties of merchantability or fitness of use for a particular purpose. Neither the author nor the publisher shall be held liable or responsible to any person or entity with respect to any loss or incidental or consequential damages caused, or alleged to have been caused, directly or indirectly, by the information contained or stored in this book. No part of this book should be construed as providing specific advice relating to proper password selection and/or the implementation of security policy and practices.

The recommendations expressed in this book are based upon the current knowledge and understanding of "best practices" by the authors and contributors. These recommendations are not claimed to be comprehensive or complete or even necessarily correct in all circumstances.

$\mathcal{W}$here to keep this book.

This book is only as secure as you make it. Consider using this book as your primary, secondary, or backup password storage resource. The book is recommended as a component to an overall password storage strategy.

 *This book should always be stored in a secure place such as a locked desk drawer or safe.*

If found, please contact:

name: _____

email: _____

home phone: _____

mobile phone: _____

work phone: _____

$\mathscr{P}$assword Security.

In the Digital Age, your personal password and information security should be one of your top priorities. According to Forbes, in 2008, over 10 million individuals were defrauded of over $48 billion dollars. That amount is expected to rise exponentially in the coming years.

Prior to the mid 1990's, the average user only needed a few passwords to go about living their life securely. Today, the same individual may be required to maintain hundreds of passwords.

Everything from shopping to banking and paying bills online now requires a password. Unfortunately, most people continue to use the same password over and over again. This practice is incredibly dangerous and exposes them to becoming a victim of crimes ranging from credit card fraud to identity theft. The need for secure passwords is increasingly important.

The purpose of this book is to heighten your awareness regarding password security. It provides fundamental considerations for creating complex passwords and provides practical methods to help keep you safe online.

 *Always keep a written backup of your passwords, like this book, in a locked and secured place.*

Don't get Phished.

Phishing is a method cybercriminals use to gain access to your account, personal information, or computer. Cybercriminals often use e-mail and direct phone contact to phish for information. The phisher might say they are calling you from your bank or credit card security department. Most recently, these crooks have been saying they are with technical support from Microsoft® and other recognizable companies. They can be very convincing and will use fear tactics to gain your confidence.

While your bank security department may call you to advise you of possible fraudulent activity; they will NEVER ask for your password, address, credit card information, social security number, or any other personal information. Your bank knows who you are, where you live, and all of your pertinent information. If your credit card or online account has been compromised, they don't need your credit card verification code, card number, online username, or password. Don't give ANY information to anyone who is calling you. Never click on e-mail links, allegedly provided by your bank, advising your password has expired or been compromised.

Companies like Microsoft®, Yahoo®, and Google® do not call people to tell them their account has been compromised. Never allow someone who calls you to have remote access to your computer. Lastly, the IT Department at your company will never call you and ask for your username or password. But if you have given it to someone, you better call your IT Department and let them know promptly.

 *Emails which advise your account has been compromised are almost certainly phishing scams. Never click on the links provided!*

Give your password to no one.

If you have ever disclosed your password, it should be changed promptly. Your vendors don't need your password to access your account and they will never call you to ask for it. It is important to note that email and telephone caller ID information can be manipulated by criminals. This is a method called spoofing.

Don't simply trust someone because your caller ID shows "YOURBANK" or something generic like "SECURITY DEPT."

Some vendors require a PIN number to verify your identity; this is not generally the same as your password.

Vendors, *especially banks*, will NEVER call you and ask you to verify or confirm your password.

 *Never provide your password, PIN number, or username to anyone who has called you or contacted you via email.*

*W*hat you should never use!

The rule is, "If a password is easy for you to remember, it is easy for cybercriminals to try." Using common sayings, dates, names, and words are easily cracked. If you are using them, you should consider changing them immediately.

- "password" is not a password
- Your birthdate "012655", or any date, is not acceptable.
- Simple numerical combinations are not safe; "123", "456", etc.
- Sports teams like "Lakers", "Steelers", etc. are easily cracked and commonly used.
- Your child's or spouse's name is easily cracked; "suzy", "suzy123", etc. should never be used.
- QWERTY passwords are passwords based upon various keyboard arrangements. They may seem to be complex, but hackers are very familiar with the various keyboard arrangements.
- Your favorite bible verse is the hacker's favorite too, "john316", "romans109", etc.
- Passwords like "abc456" are ridiculously easy to guess and can be generated sequentially by a hackers simple computer bots.
- Passwords including the words "Monkey", "trustno1", "letmein" are increasingly popular. Don't use them!

 ***Using the same password for everything is neither a strategy, nor a solution. Don't do it!***

Password Storage.

Users often store their passwords in one or more of the following locations:

1. Under their keyboard
2. On sticky notes attached to their computer
3. In their wallet
4. Other non-secure locations
5. On their computer in text files with a filename of password.doc or passwords.txt.

None of these locations should be considered secure. They are the first place a thief will look, and they should be considered compromised. If prying eyes can easily see the password affixed to your computer, you should assume someone else has it written down and may have access to your information.

A good example of a potential compromise is a neighbor or service repairman who has been in your home at some point.

 *If you have been infected by MALWARE or a virus, you should have your system looked at by a certified professional to ensure it is clean.*

The same for simplicity.

Despite many well publicized instances of major websites having been hacked, nearly 50% of all computer users continue to use only a few passwords. There are many opinions about making some passwords the same, but you should never do it.

An example might be keeping all of your social networking site passwords the same for simplicity. If a hacker figures out your Facebook® password, his or her next stop is LinkedIn® and all of the other popular social networking sites. The more information a hacker can collect about you, the more likely he can steal your identity or access accounts of greater importance. It isn't a good idea to keep any passwords the same.

 *Many websites will assign you a default password at sign-up, don't forget to change it to something secure.*

*W*hat about my login/username?

In a perfect world, login/usernames would be as complex as passwords. The most secure online sites have implemented such policies. However, it has become increasingly popular for website administrators to use your email address as your login/username. With this, 50% of the equation is already compromised.

E-mail addresses are quickly collected by spammers and hackers through MALWARE, viruses, and access to your friends' compromised accounts. Essentially, if ANYONE else knows or stores your email address in their system, the spammers and hackers already have it. This makes keeping your passwords secure even more important.

If you have the ability to create a login/username for your online account, it is a best practice to use something moderately complex. Follow the same rules of "What you should never use!" Consider something like CS943JC2 instead of myname@somedomain.com.

***Common words are NOT passwords!
If they are in any dictionary, they have
already been compromised!***

*W*hat is a good password???

The fact is that over 90% of us are not implementing password best practices in one or more of our online accounts. Start changing your passwords to something more complex today. Consider using these best practices.

Strong passwords are a combination of length, complexity, case, variation and variety. Think random!

1. Use non-predictive or disordered methodology when creating passwords.
2. Passwords should always be at least 6 characters long, 8 or more characters are better.
3. Vowels can be replaced with numbers.
4. Alternate case: "LoVe" vs "Love", but "love" anything should never be used.
5. Use a combination of numbers and letters in a non-predictive sequence. Examples. "iiksmW17" or "UkmQBrY8" are not words or a predictive sequence.
6. Consider using the vanity plate rule. Take your phrase and squeeze it into 8 or more characters with numbers, caps and small letters, and special characters.

 *In the rare occasion you share your password with someone, like your IT support technician, change it promptly to ensure restricted access.*

Tools to create complex password.

If you are like most, creating complex passwords is a difficult task. Consider using an online password generator to create passwords.

Be very careful when searching for websites which create passwords, as they too could be a source for computer infection or password compromise.

Visit www.tekeaseonsite.com/passwords for links to known safe online password generation tools and software.

 *Even the strongest passwords are no good if they aren't a secret.*
Don't share your passwords!

*M*y complex password rotation secret

Rotating the same passwords isn't good enough. You can use my complex password rotation secret to add to your ALREADY COMPLEX password for many months.

As an example, I will start with the phase "I like jelly donuts too", which I do! Using capital letters, lowercase letters, special characters, and numbers for some vowels, I create…

"iL1K3j3llyD0nuTs@"

This password would take a desktop PC about 71 quadrillion years to crack. So it is pretty secure. In 90 days I need to change my password. I don't want to have to come up with something completely different. I will take my already complex "iL1K3j3llyD0nuTs@" and apply a series of non-consecutive keystrokes I can easily remember.

"iL1K3j3llyD0nuTs@" and Shift 1 3 5 7

Type your complex password, then press and hold down the [SHIFT] key while typing a series of non-consecutive keystrokes. In my example, this produces a new password of "iL1K3j3llyD0nuTs@!#%&". The new password would take a desktop computer about 2 septillion years to crack. In 90 days, I do it again but choose a different set of [SHIFT] hold keystrokes.

This method is very handy in dealing with 90 day password requirement. However, <u>the initial password must be COMPLEX</u>. The purpose is to reduce the need to completely change a complex password, while still maintaining its complexity.

Password Storage Programs.

There are numerous software programs which can and should be used for quick access to your complex passwords. These programs are generally very easy to learn and can be invaluable if you have many passwords to maintain.

While there are many choices, both free and paid, you should look for a program which stores the password database in a secure or encrypted manner. The programs should require a master password for entry. Make sure the master password is complex!

Make sure to back-up the database in a secure method away from your primary hard-drive. We recommend keeping a periodic backup on a USB flash drive in a safe in addition to using an online backup service to help ensure you don't lose your passwords.

Links to several free and paid password storage programs are available at www.tekeaseonsite.com/passwords

 ***Never use your name, username, birthdate, child's name, alma mater, hobby, or any word that can be found in any known dictionary.***

$\mathcal{F}$inal Points and Reminders.

1. Never share your passwords with anyone.
2. Don't use the same password for anything, ever!
3. Don't rotate your passwords. Just change them.
4. Use a secure method to store your passwords.
5. Change your passwords frequently. Every 90 days is recommended. Every six months at a minimum.
6. Never access online accounts from public computers. Keystroke logging software can be used behind the scenes to capture even the most complex passwords.
7. Don't allow other people to use your computer. This includes friends and family. If they inadvertently infect your computer with MALWARE or a virus, all of your passwords must be changed.
8. Don't allow web browsers to store your password for convenience. Some MALWARE and computer viruses have been effective in capturing this information.
9. Change your passwords immediately if you even think they might have been compromised.
10. Require a password to access your computer operating system.
11. The LOGOUT button is there for a reason. Use it!
12. Teach your friends and family about the importance of password security.

You should change your passwords every 90 days. Every 6 months at a minimum!

ℋow to use this book.

If you are like most, using someone else's organizational ideas can be difficult to implement. This is why most organizers and day planners never get fully implemented by the purchaser. Mostly, these expensive organizational tools just collect dust while waiting for future implementation of grand organizational plans.

This password organizer is simple to use by design. While separating passwords alphabetically, by group, purpose, etc., may seem like a brilliant idea; most people are simply unable to remember how they organized them later. This is why there are no tabs, indexes, or groups in this book.

Keep it simple! Don't skip pages in an attempt to separate or organize your passwords. List them one right after the other until you fill the page. If you title your passwords accordingly, you will have no trouble finding them when you need them.

title:	(USE INK)
login/username:	(USE INK)
password:	(USE PENCIL)
website/URL:	(USE PENCIL)
date expires:	(USE PENCIL)
date changed:	(USE PENCIL)
security answers:	(USE PENCIL
notes/PIN number:	(USE PENCIL)

title:
_____

login/username:
_____

password:
_____

website/URL:
_____

date expires:
_____

date changed:
_____

security answers:
_____

notes/PIN number:
_____

title:
_____

login/username:
_____

password:
_____

website/URL:
_____

date expires:
_____

date changed:
_____

security answers:
_____

notes/PIN number:
_____

title:
_____

login/username:
_____

password:
_____

website/URL:
_____

date expires:
_____

date changed:
_____

security answers:
_____

notes/PIN number:
_____

title:

login/username:

password:

website/URL:

date expires:

date changed:

security answers:

notes/PIN number:

title:

login/username:

password:

website/URL:

date expires:

date changed:

security answers:

notes/PIN number:

title:

login/username:

password:

website/URL:

date expires:

date changed:

security answers:

notes/PIN number:

title:

login/username:

password:

website/URL:

date expires:

date changed:

security answers:

notes/PIN number:

title:

login/username:

password:

website/URL:

date expires:

date changed:

security answers:

notes/PIN number:

title:

login/username:

password:

website/URL:

date expires:

date changed:

security answers:

notes/PIN number:

title:

login/username:

password:

website/URL:

date expires:

date changed:

security answers:

notes/PIN number:

title:

login/username:

password:

website/URL:

date expires:

date changed:

security answers:

notes/PIN number:

title:

login/username:

password:

website/URL:

date expires:

date changed:

security answers:

notes/PIN number:

title:
login/username:
password:
website/URL:
date expires:
date changed:
security answers:

notes/PIN number:

---

title:
login/username:
password:
website/URL:
date expires:
date changed:
security answers:

notes/PIN number:

---

title:
login/username:
password:
website/URL:
date expires:
date changed:
security answers:

notes/PIN number:

title:

login/username:

password:

website/URL:

date expires:

date changed:

security answers:

notes/PIN number:

title:

login/username:

password:

website/URL:

date expires:

date changed:

security answers:

notes/PIN number:

title:

login/username:

password:

website/URL:

date expires:

date changed:

security answers:

notes/PIN number:

title:
_____
login/username:
_____
password:
_____
website/URL:
_____
date expires:
_____
date changed:
_____
security answers:
_____

notes/PIN number:
_____

title:
_____
login/username:
_____
password:
_____
website/URL:
_____
date expires:
_____
date changed:
_____
security answers:
_____

notes/PIN number:
_____

title:
_____
login/username:
_____
password:
_____
website/URL:
_____
date expires:
_____
date changed:
_____
security answers:
_____

notes/PIN number:
_____

title:

login/username:

password:

website/URL:

date expires:

date changed:

security answers:

notes/PIN number:

title:

login/username:

password:

website/URL:

date expires:

date changed:

security answers:

notes/PIN number:

title:

login/username:

password:

website/URL:

date expires:

date changed:

security answers:

notes/PIN number:

title:

login/username:

password:

website/URL:

date expires:

date changed:

security answers:

notes/PIN number:

---

title:

login/username:

password:

website/URL:

date expires:

date changed:

security answers:

notes/PIN number:

---

title:

login/username:

password:

website/URL:

date expires:

date changed:

security answers:

notes/PIN number:

title:

login/username:

password:

website/URL:

date expires:

date changed:

security answers:

notes/PIN number:

---

title:

login/username:

password:

website/URL:

date expires:

date changed:

security answers:

notes/PIN number:

---

title:

login/username:

password:

website/URL:

date expires:

date changed:

security answers:

notes/PIN number:

---

title:

login/username:

password:

website/URL:

date expires:

date changed:

security answers:

notes/PIN number:

---

title:

login/username:

password:

website/URL:

date expires:

date changed:

security answers:

notes/PIN number:

---

title:

login/username:

password:

website/URL:

date expires:

date changed:

security answers:

notes/PIN number:

title:
_____
login/username:
_____
password:
_____
website/URL:
_____
date expires:
_____
date changed:
_____
security answers:
_____

notes/PIN number:
_____

title:
_____
login/username:
_____
password:
_____
website/URL:
_____
date expires:
_____
date changed:
_____
security answers:
_____

notes/PIN number:
_____

title:
_____
login/username:
_____
password:
_____
website/URL:
_____
date expires:
_____
date changed:
_____
security answers:
_____

notes/PIN number:
_____

title:

login/username:

password:

website/URL:

date expires:

date changed:

security answers:

notes/PIN number:

---

title:

login/username:

password:

website/URL:

date expires:

date changed:

security answers:

notes/PIN number:

---

title:

login/username:

password:

website/URL:

date expires:

date changed:

security answers:

notes/PIN number:

---

title:

login/username:

password:

website/URL:

date expires:

date changed:

security answers:

notes/PIN number:

title:

login/username:

password:

website/URL:

date expires:

date changed:

security answers:

notes/PIN number:

title:

login/username:

password:

website/URL:

date expires:

date changed:

security answers:

notes/PIN number:

title:

login/username:

password:

website/URL:

date expires:

date changed:

security answers:

notes/PIN number:

---

title:

login/username:

password:

website/URL:

date expires:

date changed:

security answers:

notes/PIN number:

---

title:

login/username:

password:

website/URL:

date expires:

date changed:

security answers:

notes/PIN number:

---

title:

login/username:

password:

website/URL:

date expires:

date changed:

security answers:

notes/PIN number:

---

title:

login/username:

password:

website/URL:

date expires:

date changed:

security answers:

notes/PIN number:

---

title:

login/username:

password:

website/URL:

date expires:

date changed:

security answers:

notes/PIN number:

title:

login/username:

password:

website/URL:

date expires:

date changed:

security answers:

notes/PIN number:

---

title:

login/username:

password:

website/URL:

date expires:

date changed:

security answers:

notes/PIN number:

---

title:

login/username:

password:

website/URL:

date expires:

date changed:

security answers:

notes/PIN number:

---

title:

login/username:

password:

website/URL:

date expires:

date changed:

security answers:

notes/PIN number:

title:

login/username:

password:

website/URL:

date expires:

date changed:

security answers:

notes/PIN number:

title:

login/username:

password:

website/URL:

date expires:

date changed:

security answers:

notes/PIN number:

title:
login/username:
password:
website/URL:
date expires:
date changed:
security answers:

notes/PIN number:

title:
login/username:
password:
website/URL:
date expires:
date changed:
security answers:

notes/PIN number:

title:
login/username:
password:
website/URL:
date expires:
date changed:
security answers:

notes/PIN number:

title:

login/username:

password:

website/URL:

date expires:

date changed:

security answers:

notes/PIN number:

title:

login/username:

password:

website/URL:

date expires:

date changed:

security answers:

notes/PIN number:

title:

login/username:

password:

website/URL:

date expires:

date changed:

security answers:

notes/PIN number:

title:
_____

login/username:
_____

password:
_____

website/URL:
_____

date expires:
_____

date changed:
_____

security answers:
_____

notes/PIN number:
_____

title:
_____

login/username:
_____

password:
_____

website/URL:
_____

date expires:
_____

date changed:
_____

security answers:
_____

notes/PIN number:
_____

title:
_____

login/username:
_____

password:
_____

website/URL:
_____

date expires:
_____

date changed:
_____

security answers:
_____

notes/PIN number:
_____

title:

login/username:

password:

website/URL:

date expires:

date changed:

security answers:

notes/PIN number:

title:

login/username:

password:

website/URL:

date expires:

date changed:

security answers:

notes/PIN number:

title:

login/username:

password:

website/URL:

date expires:

date changed:

security answers:

notes/PIN number:

title:

login/username:

password:

website/URL:

date expires:

date changed:

security answers:

notes/PIN number:

---

title:

login/username:

password:

website/URL:

date expires:

date changed:

security answers:

notes/PIN number:

---

title:

login/username:

password:

website/URL:

date expires:

date changed:

security answers:

notes/PIN number:

title:

login/username:

password:

website/URL:

date expires:

date changed:

security answers:

notes/PIN number:

title:

login/username:

password:

website/URL:

date expires:

date changed:

security answers:

notes/PIN number:

title:

login/username:

password:

website/URL:

date expires:

date changed:

security answers:

notes/PIN number:

title:

login/username:

password:

website/URL:

date expires:

date changed:

security answers:

notes/PIN number:

---

title:

login/username:

password:

website/URL:

date expires:

date changed:

security answers:

notes/PIN number:

---

title:

login/username:

password:

website/URL:

date expires:

date changed:

security answers:

notes/PIN number:

---

title:

login/username:

password:

website/URL:

date expires:

date changed:

security answers:

notes/PIN number:

---

title:

login/username:

password:

website/URL:

date expires:

date changed:

security answers:

notes/PIN number:

---

title:

login/username:

password:

website/URL:

date expires:

date changed:

security answers:

notes/PIN number:

title:

login/username:

password:

website/URL:

date expires:

date changed:

security answers:

notes/PIN number:

title:

login/username:

password:

website/URL:

date expires:

date changed:

security answers:

notes/PIN number:

title:

login/username:

password:

website/URL:

date expires:

date changed:

security answers:

notes/PIN number:

title:

login/username:

password:

website/URL:

date expires:

date changed:

security answers:

notes/PIN number:

title:

login/username:

password:

website/URL:

date expires:

date changed:

security answers:

notes/PIN number:

title:

login/username:

password:

website/URL:

date expires:

date changed:

security answers:

notes/PIN number:

title:

login/username:

password:

website/URL:

date expires:

date changed:

security answers:

notes/PIN number:

---

title:

login/username:

password:

website/URL:

date expires:

date changed:

security answers:

notes/PIN number:

---

title:

login/username:

password:

website/URL:

date expires:

date changed:

security answers:

notes/PIN number:

---

title:

login/username:

password:

website/URL:

date expires:

date changed:

security answers:

notes/PIN number:

---

title:

login/username:

password:

website/URL:

date expires:

date changed:

security answers:

notes/PIN number:

---

title:

login/username:

password:

website/URL:

date expires:

date changed:

security answers:

notes/PIN number:

---

title:
_____

login/username:
_____

password:
_____

website/URL:
_____

date expires:
_____

date changed:
_____

security answers:
_____

notes/PIN number:
_____

---

title:
_____

login/username:
_____

password:
_____

website/URL:
_____

date expires:
_____

date changed:
_____

security answers:
_____

notes/PIN number:
_____

---

title:
_____

login/username:
_____

password:
_____

website/URL:
_____

date expires:
_____

date changed:
_____

security answers:
_____

notes/PIN number:
_____

---

title:

login/username:

password:

website/URL:

date expires:

date changed:

security answers:

notes/PIN number:

---

title:

login/username:

password:

website/URL:

date expires:

date changed:

security answers:

notes/PIN number:

---

title:

login/username:

password:

website/URL:

date expires:

date changed:

security answers:

notes/PIN number:

title:

login/username:

password:

website/URL:

date expires:

date changed:

security answers:

notes/PIN number:

---

title:

login/username:

password:

website/URL:

date expires:

date changed:

security answers:

notes/PIN number:

---

title:

login/username:

password:

website/URL:

date expires:

date changed:

security answers:

notes/PIN number:

---

title:

login/username:

password:

website/URL:

date expires:

date changed:

security answers:

notes/PIN number:

---

title:

login/username:

password:

website/URL:

date expires:

date changed:

security answers:

notes/PIN number:

---

title:

login/username:

password:

website/URL:

date expires:

date changed:

security answers:

notes/PIN number:

---

title:

login/username:

password:

website/URL:

date expires:

date changed:

security answers:

notes/PIN number:

---

title:

login/username:

password:

website/URL:

date expires:

date changed:

security answers:

notes/PIN number:

---

title:

login/username:

password:

website/URL:

date expires:

date changed:

security answers:

notes/PIN number:

title:

login/username:

password:

website/URL:

date expires:

date changed:

security answers:

notes/PIN number:

title:

login/username:

password:

website/URL:

date expires:

date changed:

security answers:

notes/PIN number:

title:

login/username:

password:

website/URL:

date expires:

date changed:

security answers:

notes/PIN number:

Home Wireless Private Network Information

SSID/wireless network name:

router IP address:

router PIN:

passphrase:

shared key/network key:

login username:

login password:

date last changed:

Home Wireless Guest Network Information

SSID/wireless network name:

passphrase:

shared key/network key:

login username:

login password:

date last changed:

E-mail Server Information

email address:

mail server type:

incoming server/port:

outgoing server/port:

username:

password:

date last changed:

Internet Service Provider

company name: _____

account number: _____

provider website/URL: _____

support phone number: _____

webmail website/URL: _____

call in PIN number: _____

contract expiration date: _____

static IP address: _____

Technical Support Provider

company name: _____

support phone number: _____

provider website/URL: _____

client portal website/URL: _____

call in PIN number: _____

contract expiration date: _____

Important Phone Numbers

_____

_____

_____

_____

_____

_____

_____

_____

_____

_____

*H*elpful Online Resources

Password Guidance
> www.tekeaseonsite.com/passwords

How Secure is Your Password
> www.howsecureismypassword.net

Password Meter
> www.passwordmeter.com

ID Theft Protection
> www.tekeaseonsite.com/idlock

Identity Theft Task Force
> www.idtheft.gov

Federal Trade Commission
> www.ftc.gov/idtheft

Internet Crime Complain Center
> www.ic3.gov

Glossary

Adware Computer software loaded into system memory with the sole intention of displaying unwanted advertisements, like pop-up ads. Many adware programs will now also play unwanted audio commercials through the computer speakers. Adware does not usually spread from one computer to another without human intervention.

Cookies A cookie is a small file placed on a computer when visiting websites. The file helps identify a particular computer system to a particular website. Cookies are used by nearly all website administrators today. Many banks and other organizations now require cookies to be enabled to identify a client authorized computer to gain access to online information.

Cybercriminal An individual engaged in crime that involves computers, networks, and other connected communication devices.

Hacker An individual who uses developed or acquired knowledge of computer system hardware or software to circumvent intended security measures or procedures. The term is also often used to describe computer hobbyists or programmers not actually engaged in criminal activity.

IT Information Technology. The group responsible for information systems within an organization.

Malware Malicious software which interferes with normal computer operations and invokes procedures without the system operator's knowledge or permission. Malware can be used by cybercriminals for a variety of purposes. Many malware programs are designed to confuse the system operator about the presence of their virus protection. The malware may produce endless messages purporting the computer is infected with viruses, or advise of pending hard-drive failure. Malware infections are often implemented via a Trojan horse method. Malware does not usually spread from one computer to another without human intervention.

Passphrase   A passphrase was intended to simplify wireless connectivity and authentication between a device and the wireless network. Passphrases are part of networks which use WEP encryption. The passphrase is used to generate a series of hexadecimal keys which are shared between network devices. WEP encryption has serious known security weaknesses and should no longer be used.

Phishing   An unlawful method of sending emails purporting to be from a legitimate company in an effort to obtain personal or confidential information from the recipient.

PIN   Personal Identification Number

Shared Key   A case sensitive password used by a computer or wireless device to gain access to a wireless network.

Spoofing   E-mail spoofing is a technique cybercriminals use to forge the e-mail header or sender address of an e-mail to make the message appear as if is coming from a trusted source.

Spyware   Computer software created to collect personal and confidential information about the system operator. Spyware most often sends the collected information to the author of the software. Spyware does not usually spread from one computer to another without human intervention.

SSID   Service Set Identifier on a wireless network. A case sensitive name used by a computer or other wireless device to locate a specific wireless network access point or router.

Virus   Computer software created by cybercriminals for a variety of nefarious purposes. Most computer viruses are intended to cause actual harm, like hard-drive or operating system failure, to the computer. Viruses usually attempt to spread from one computer to another using a variety of methods. A worm virus will propagate across a computer network one machine to the next.

About TEKEASE ON-SITE®.

TEKEASE ON-SITE® is a nationwide technology service provider of computer repair and technology services to residential clients and small business.

TEKEASE ON-SITE provides:
- Helpdesk Services
- Remote Diagnosis and Repair
- Antivirus Protection and SPAM Filtering
- Hosted Microsoft® Exchange Services
- Remote System Monitoring and Management
- Domain Registration
- Website Design, Management and Hosting
- Internet Family Safety
- Training and Consulting Services
- Telephone Systems and Services

Follow TEKEASE ON-SITE® on Twitter® @tekeaseonsite, on Facebook® at www.facebook.com/tekease, or on the web at www.tekeaseonsite.com.

Contact

TEKEASE ON-SITE
P.O. Box 3501
Peoria, IL 61612-3501

Phone: 309.689.8355
Fax: 309.222.8894
www.tekeaseonsite.com
support@tekeaseonsite.com

About the Author

Corbett Speciale is a tech-savvy entrepreneur, sales leader, and small business expert. His background includes nearly three decades in information technology, professional sales, and small business leadership. Corbett has held positions with Caterpillar®, AT&T® and Polycom®. He has advised state governments, educational institutions, Fortune 500 companies, and hundreds of other organizations regarding business operations, communications, and technology best practices. Corbett is a former Special Agent Criminal Investigator for the Department of Defense where he investigated numerous felony computer and Internet related crimes.

Corbett holds Bachelor's Degree in Accounting and is a cybercrime specialist who advocates for family safety through training, consulting, and education. Corbett is a sought after public speaker at conferences regarding small business, Internet safety, and technology.

Corbett is available for speaking engagements regarding small business, technology best practices, Internet safety, and sales team development.

Follow Corbett Speciale on Twitter® @corbettspeciale or on the web at www.corbettspeciale.com.

Contact

Corbett Speciale @corbettspeciale
P.O. Box 3501 www.corbettspeciale.com
Peoria, IL 61612-3501

www.ingramcontent.com/pod-product-compliance
Lightning Source LLC
Chambersburg PA
CBHW051244170526
45165CB00004B/1576